STRATEGIES
For Saving The Next
GENERATION

by David Burrows

PNEUMA LIFE

PUBLISHING

Strategies for Saving the Next Generation

Published by:

PUBLISHING

Printed in the United States of America

Copyright ©1994
David Burrows
P.O. Box N-9583
Nassau, Bahamas

Strategies For Saving the Next Generation
ISBN 1-56229-403-2
$5.95 Soft Cover

Pneuma Life Publishing
P.O. Box 10612
Bakersfield, CA 93389
(805) 837-2113

Contents

Dedication
Acknowledgments
Foreword
Preface

Dedication

This book is dedicated to all those who stand in the trenches, reaching the youth of today, who are so often lost and without hope or direction. My partners in "Crime," Fairest "The Doctor" Hill, Steve Wiley, Zhivargo Laing, System 3, Ron Luce, Teen Challenge Bahamas including GO & Fox, Rick and Greg, Lester "Positive" Lewis, the entire Live Youth crew and the BFM directors and fellowship. People I have worked with to rescue, teach, train and develop youth into citizens of the KOG (Kingdom of God).

Acknowledgments

It's been a long time since I walked down the aisle of that little church in the Commanche Park Housing Project in Tulsa, Oklahoma, and gave my life to Jesus Christ. Although it was not my intention to get saved at that time, the Lord was calling me. The more I looked for excuses, the less valid ones I found for not giving my life to him.

There were ups and downs in the beginning. I did not understand much about this new life, but I knew I would not go back to the drugs, the violence and aimless sex of the days before. I knew I had to take this message to the street. I knew that God was asking me to return to people I left behind late in my teen years. I knew he was saying that my work would be with the youth.

I thank God for those who encouraged me along the way, Robyn Gool, who kept me in line when I started to stray. I cannot forget those days in the little churches all over Oklahoma and North Carolina. Dave Lamb and Pastor Curry at Evangelistic Temple. Myles Munroe in Nassau, Bahamas who lives helping others fulfill their purpose and potential, and all the others who have said encouraging words along the way. Derwin Stewart, who is "potential in fifth gear," and who assisted so much in getting this project to its completion.

As always, I am thankful to God for giving me a wife called Angie and wonderful children like Arri and Davreille, who remind me every day that there must be a God. Thank you all for helping this book to come out of me.

Foreword

"What is wrong with these young people, why can't they behave!" If, as a pastor, you have ever uttered those words, then your very acknowledgment of these sentiments validates the need for a Youth Ministry.

The teenage years are a period of rapid transition, character formation, and a constant flow of energy. Most of our church formats, do not necessarily cater to the needs of the youth, and if there is not a deliberate effort to reach them where they are at and with the language they understand, we may very well lose them.

The Youth Ministry is a vital link between the present and the future. Remember that those "troublesome" youth of today are the leaders of tomorrow, both in the church and community. The Youth Ministry gives direction and meaning to the tremendous energy, drive and talents of the youth of the congregation. The Youth Ministry develops Godlike character and integrity by utilizing the language of the youth. One of the benefits of the Youth Ministry is to mobilize the youth into meaningful ministry, fulfillment of the vision of the ministry, and outreach.

If you are serious about utilizing all of your human resources, preparing future leaders, character development, and affecting the next generation, then this book is not an option, but a necessity.

Richard H. Pinder
Pastor / Teacher
Bahamas Faith Ministries

Preface

One of the tragedies of today, is the fact that youth are often an afterthought and many times are left out of the planning of the ordinary church. Sometimes there is no budget for youth, sometimes there is no tolerance, sometimes Youth Ministry is a lonely place because Pastors and church members forget them. But they will not go away, because if they do, our churches have no future.

That same young man with the ear ring in his ear, and that lady with the mini skirt on, will be in charge of your church someday. If we can get past the temporal things, we can get to the eternal and do the job God has called us to do where youth are concerned. We can see problems or see potential. If we see problems, then we create a "bless us" club for the chosen few. If we see potential, then we create an avenue for much greater ministry in the future.

This book was written to assist those who dare to work with youth, and care enough to believe like Jesus believed, about youth. Who does not know that change hardly ever takes place "over the hill." This book is written for those who will go into this frontier and bring the message, home to a generation that is waiting for someone to tell them the truth.

My hope is that if you do not have a youth ministry at your church, this book will serve as the starting point to help you get on the move. If you have already started, I hope that you find the information you need to be more effective. Whatever position you may be in, I believe you will find something in the pages that follow that will help to change the way you do business as a Pastor, Youth Pastor, youth worker or one who helps along the way.

Let's get busy in obedience to the Lord Jesus said (Matt. 28:19 & 20). Teach the children, reach the youth by any means or methods necessary. He left the method up to us. He just gave the message. Let's do it right.

Peace.....Dave Burrows....

Chapter 1

Why Have a Youth Ministry Anyway?

Youth Ministry....who needs one anyway? Many churches, pastors and others wonder, "Why in the world do we need a youth ministry in the first place? Do they need special attention? Shouldn't they be able to relate as adults and sit under teachings? Why should we have a separate meeting for youth? We already have enough meetings as it is!"

These are very important questions that someone must answer soon, or we may find ourselves in a position where the church is an organization that is in touch with the last generation, but severely out of touch with this one.

It is interesting to note, that as history bears it out, relatively few advancements or changes in the world have taken place as a result of a mass movement of senior citizens. Yet every generation of Youth ushers in new ideas and enthusiasm that produces changes that affect the world for years to come. The church is no different. Our teenagers of today will be either in a position of leadership within the church, or they will be making a contribution to society as leaders in unrelated fields, or as leaders in the fight against the church.

The fact is, if we do not make a concerted effort to reach our youth, they will be and are being reached by others, whether it be the rock musician, the politician, the drug dealer, the gang member or the enemies of God.

It is an unfortunate fact of life that most Pastors, especially older Pastors, are almost totally out of touch with the youth of today. Many of them don't even see the need to be aware, or to have someone on their staff who is in touch. Some very large churches have no department or full time staff designated for youth. Some churches have no sports program, no recreation program, no teaching on their level and no participation of youth in the affairs of the church.

Sometimes the attitude is, "Shouldn't we just tell them to sit and listen like everyone else and be quiet and stay out of the way?" The truth is, if we tell them to stay out of our way, they probably will. They will leave and go off into a world that is only too inviting, with destruction carefully packaged for them.

The Youth in today's world are quite different, even as the world is different. They grow up in a decidedly different environment. Many in this generation do not know what a real family is. So many grow up in one parent homes, or homes confused by the distortions of the "modern family." Single parents, step parents, homosexual parents, foster parents and the list goes on.

Youth today are indelibly influenced by a number of factors, bigger and more complicated problems exist in our communities than have ever been seen before. More divorces, more sexual abuse, more domestic violence, more murders, more hypocrisy, more cynicism, more unbelief.....more, more, more. You name it and our youth today are experiencing more of it.

By the same token, they are experiencing less and less of what they need. Less love, less real family life, less honesty, less compassion, less caring, less attention, less concern and less truth. It would be nice, and it would be very convenient to have the attitude that they will sort themselves out, but it is not practical. You need a youth ministry in your church. Without a youth ministry, you may end up allowing gangs to be the youth ministries you lack in your church.

Teenagers are the fastest growing group and largest carriers of AIDS. There are over 90,000 gang members in Los Angeles alone. Your young people are being lured by musical evangelists, gang evangelists, sex evangelists and whatever is being offered in the marketplace. The majority of youth in the world do not go to church.

In America, it is said that the number of youth attending church has declined from 40% 20 years ago, to less than 10% today. Young people are having more abortions, using more drugs and getting pregnant at a higher rate now, than ever before. Our youth are more violent, believe less in God and care less about political matters than ever before. We need a youth ministry in every church.

Some statistics indicate that, 85% of people who get saved do so before the age of 19. Look back on your life. What happened during your teenage years? Did you get saved before you were an adult? Youth are too important for us to haphazardly plan their entry into the Kingdom of God, or to not plan it at all. Your young people need specific attention, which if they don't receive it they will not be there tomorrow.

One unfortunate circumstance is that youth will not get the gospel by osmosis. You cannot present the gospel to toddlers the same way you would present it to adults, because the make up of a toddler suggests that they learn differently. You may say to a toddler, "Sit down while I recite from the King James version of the Bible and preach for one hour and a half.

Before you properly begin the toddlers will be flying imaginary kites and driving imaginary cars. Obviously they have different needs. Sometimes, because of the physical size of teenagers, we assume that they have the same needs and concerns and can be communicated to in the same manner as adults. This is not true at all.

The primary concern of an adult may be paying the bills or preparing for a new career move. The primary concern of a teenager may be that his girlfriend or her boyfriend didn't call last night, or whether or not to engage in sex for the first time. The concerns of young people are short term, yet they feel the same pain of adults.

Your problem may be big to you, and you may look at the teenager and say their problem is not that big. Their problem is just as big to them as yours is to you. We must address their concerns, one on one, from the Bible, the same way we address our concerns.

Chapter 2

Priorities In Youth Ministry

REACHING OUT TO YOUTH

It is important to minister to youth and their needs on their level, and to touch the things that concern them. Their needs are unique to them. To give you an example, many young boys, and to some extent girls, are interested in sports, yet many churches have no sporting facilities or program.

Every church should have a gym, basketball court or other sporting facility, because that is where many young people are at. If you think about what they learn at the neighborhood park, you will appreciate the necessity of church sporting facilities.

I grew up on the basketball court and what I learned there helped to set my course in life. I learned to fight, get high on drugs and alcohol, swear, gamble and take advantage of women. That was the nature of my schooling on the basketball court.

As we look around our world, one unfortunate thing that you will notice, is that many 'neighborhood' parks have been taken over by gangs, homeless people and any variety of social deviates, who make it unsafe for your children to play ball. This presents a golden opportunity for churches. Invite them to play ball at your church, where they will learn truth and much better values.

In reaching youth, we have to ask what are youth into. You cannot reach youth by presenting them something they are not interested in.

The message of the gospel cannot change, but the method through which it is presented can and should change, even as times and seasons change.

One thing almost all young people are into is music. They may not like the same music you do, but you can be assured that they are into music. Rock music and Rap music happen to be some of the most popular mediums of the day. If that's the language of "Rome" then speak it to reach the "Romans." Take your message to your young people in the form they are most likely to listen to.

Our message is not a culture or a style, it is truth which is packaged differently, according to the audience. When we are presenting the gospel to little children, they will not get excited over hymns sung in a traditional manner. They will get excited over the same hymns, if you package them in the style of music they like.

We must properly package our message for the intended audience. Too often we take traditional adult packages, and present them to unsettled, excited teenagers. It never works!

We must also address the issues that concern them. Young people are not interested in the price of gold in London, or the foreign policy of your country. They may have a slight interest in those things, but more than likely they are interested in how God relates to the things that concern them everyday. Dating, sex, drugs, peer pressure, physical beauty or talents, having a good time, music, relating to parents and the latest fashions are things young people are normally most concerned with.

Not only must we reach them, but we must motivate them to reach their friends. If we leave it up to the youth pastor, or the older church members to reach our youth, it will never happen. The Bible never said pastors should go into all the world and preach the gospel. It said 'we' referring to every believer, regardless of age, gender or social status. We must teach our youth to reach each other.

UNDERSTANDING INFLUENCING FACTORS

Youth in today's world are indelibly influenced by a number of factors....bigger and more complicated problems than we have seen before.......more divorces, sexual abuse, domestic violence, etc.. There are five major factors or groups affecting and influencing the lives of youth. Each of these affects young people differently. In some cases, they compete for the interest of our youth. Whatever the impact may be, we must thoroughly appreciate the impact of each upon the lives of our youth.

Parents

Although we may think parents don't impact the lives of teenagers, often the first, most powerful and lasting influence in their lives is that of their parents. If parents are uncaring, mean and ugly, scars are left on the child that ultimately creates the same character within. If parents are kind and fair, children normally end up acting the same way, even if they depart from it for a while.

Every youth minister must understand the role and importance of parents, and learn to work with them. They must help kids to relate to their parents better than they would have otherwise. Every youth ministry must include parents in it's planning and design.

We must communicate with, and work with parents if we are to be successful. Without proper communication with parents, a gap will exist between youth ministers, the youth they are working with, and parents. Parents trust people they know, they feel safe when you talk with them about what you are doing. Without this communication, they may end up being suspicious or apprehensive about you as a youth pastor. We must involve parents.

School

The only place teenagers are more likely to spend more time at than home, is school. In fact, many kids spend more time in school than they do at home. The friends they have at school and the teachers and the lessons they learn in school, can be just as powerful or even more powerful than the lessons they learn at home. If you are going to reach teenagers, your youth ministry must be involved in going into and reaching out to schools.

There must be a "ministry" presence in schools. One of the loneliest places in the world for a young Christian can be the classrooms, hall ways and gyms of their high schools. The state of the world is often intimidating to anyone who would stand up and say they are not interested in drugs, sex outside of marriage or engaging in activities that are in direct contradiction to the Bible. Not too many young people remain neutral when they see a Christian in school. A strong challenge by negative forces among our youth is always present in schools.

Many of the young people in your group will have to be strong and lead others in their high school or college away from the destructiveness of the day. Your young people will have to be the ones to witness, share, confront, counsel and be an example to their peers in their schools. Whatever you do your ministry must have a presence in schools.

Other Youth

Peer pressure can be the single most important force in the lives of many youth today. Often it is more important to a young person what their friends think than what their parents or pastor thinks. Kids influence each other for good or evil. Youth gangs are a good example of negative peer pressure.

Most teenagers are followers and will do what they see others do, or what seems to be popular. Our youth must be motivated to resist negative peer pressure and to exert positive peer pressure on their friends. They must be motivated enough to do the right thing.

Often, the history of Christian young people is one of being influenced and intimidated, rather than doing the influencing. Our young people must be taught to be the standard. They must be taught that they should not be intimidated by misguided teenagers they encounter on a day to day basis. They must be the ones who influence their friends for good and not for evil.

Our youth must understand that when you are right you are right, and therefore you never bow to intimidation. The three Hebrew boys in the Old Testament (Daniel 3:12) are a good example of youth who stand up for what is right, in spite of the pressures of the day.

Church

Sadly, the church is not nearly as important as it used to be. In spite of this, we still have many young people who go to church. They normally only spend an hour or two per week at church, so it is important to either increase their time in church, or to increase your influence over them while they are in church.

They want truth and desperately need it. It is the job of the church to let young people know that they have come to the right place where truth can be found. Church programming must take into account the special needs of youth, and do what is necessary to reach them, cause them to grow spiritually, and cause them to want to reach out to their friends.

If churches fail to cater to their specific needs, the world is waiting with a long list of things they should do and places they should go. This inevitably ends up leading them into the things we mentioned earlier, which so negatively impacts them.

Young people must feel that they are welcomed in your church. They cannot be seen as a nuisance or be expected to function like an adult. They must know that a special place has been prepared for them, that they are not an afterthought, and that their involvement in the life and vision in the church has been carefully planned. Facilities and equipment should reflect the needs and aspirations of today's youth, in their language and culture.

Media

As time goes on, the media takes a greater and greater role in shaping the lives of our youth. TV, movies and music probably do more to shape the morals and attitudes of this generation than any other. A great majority of today's youth acquire their values form the "tube" or the "silver screen." Many teenagers are left home by their parents with one baby sitter, the TV set. MTV, Playboy, Network soaps, these are the foster parents of our youth.

While much attention is focused on "Televangelists," evangelism never stops on television. Beer evangelism is one of the most powerful evangelistic tools of the day, "This Bud's for You" teenager ! Our musical evangelists preach the message of promiscuity, satanism and violence to teens everyday.

The movies of today introduce young people to unlimited sex, profanity and violence. On an average night of television, very little, if any, Christian values are presented to our youth. They are constantly told everybody is doing it, condoms are free, something is wrong with you if you are not sexually active. They are hammered with the message of disobedience, unstable relationships, divorce, incest, violence and the list goes on.

The media is definitely one of the most powerful forces ruling over youth. While they complain about televangelists, the most powerful televangelists are ignored and allowed to hawk their wares as they see fit. What a tragedy. We must not only advise our youth how to deal with the media, we must use the media ourselves to influence. Develop television programs, videos, radio programs, magazines and books targeted specifically for our young people.

Each of the factors noted above plays a major role in shaping the lives of our youth, thus it is important in ministering to youth to recognize where most of their time is spent, and who has the greatest influence over them. Youth ministry should include careful consideration of these five factors.

Balanced, Bible based, spiritual wisdom in these areas will guarantee good success.

CHARACTER BUILDING

One of the legacies of many modern churches is the numbers game. "My church is bigger than your church, my youth group is bigger than yours, we have a bigger parking lot, we have a bigger sanctuary, mine is bigger, mine is better," and so on.

It is much more important to be concerned with filling people in the room, rather than filling the room with people. Your ministry should focus on helping each individual to develop spirit, soul and body to the fullest extent. If you are increasing in numbers, but not seeing individual positive development, take the focus off the numbers and place it on the individuals. It is more important to feed a few youth with the word, than to have a room full of empty young people.

As a result of your youth ministry, each young person should experience and know the following:

1. Should be Born Again/Saved
2. Spirit Filled (Baptism with the Holy Spirit)
3. Good Knowledge of the Bible (basic principles and doctrines)
4. Know their purpose for living and the objectives of the Kingdom of God.

5. Should be confident, strong and bold about their faith.
6. Should be capable of being leaders in their schools or communities.
7. Should know and practice biblical standards of conduct.
8. Should be able to relate to their peers (know how to be 'cool' and not 'nerdish')
9. Should be prepared for life outside of the church walls, whether it be job, career or talents, schooling, or civic and social life.

It is important to make your youth ministry a place where young people will bring their friends who are saved and unsaved, yet discipline must be maintained. Your authority must be clearly maintained, in order to prevent the few who would like to disrupt from gaining control in your meetings. I have seen over and over in church youth groups, where a few disruptive youth have hindered the growth and development of the group. If necessary, such persons may need to be sent home if they do not improve after you have spoken to them on a one to one basis about their behavior.

PERSONAL PRIORITIES

Many times in ministry, the temptation arises where you want to give and give, work and work and try to solve every problem that you see. There is a time and a season for everything, and there are certain personal priorities that cannot be ignored or given wrong emphasis. Some of these personal priorities are:

Your relationship with God.

Your first and foremost priority in life is to your Lord and Savior Jesus Christ. You must maintain an active personal relationship with God, or you will never be truly effective in your ministry or your home life. The Bible commands that we should seek God first and that everything else will be added (Matt. 6:33). In order to maintain a proper relationship with your heavenly father you must pray, study the Word, fast and meditate on a regular basis.

All of the instruction, revelation and guidance you need must come first from your personal relationship with the Lord, before anything else. You need to hear from God yourself, in order to give proper direction to those in your care, which includes your family, the youth you work with and those who work alongside you in ministry.

Your relationship with your family.

This item is infinitely more important for the married person. If you are single, it is important to maintain a good relationship with immediate family members, although not as vitally important as a married person. Often times the tendency is for you to allow everyone else to have access to you at all times, until the people closest to you are left out, and your marriage and family relationships are impaired.

Always remember that the young people you minister to have no shortage of problems and they do need help, but you do not go home with them at the end of the day. Your wife/husband and children are where you live and sleep. Their rights must be protected. You have the responsibility of bringing your children up and of being there for your spouse, not as a visitor but as a partner in life. Make sure that you schedule your time and know how to say "no" when it is necessary. Plan for time aside with your family. Do not neglect your duties as a husband or wife for the sake of ministry.

Your Ministry

The ministry you work with is next on the priority list. The people you minister to, whom God has appointed you to work with, should occupy a high position on your list of priorities. They represent your calling and vocation in life and are the responsibility God has entrusted you with. God needs you to work with this particular group of people. They are unique for not everyone understands or cares about the things that concern them. Not everyone can communicate with or minister to them. You have been given that special assignment, so it is imperative that you take it seriously and care for them. Present them with the gospel like no one else can. Their needs are your ministry. It is important to be accessible, concerned, caring, compassionate and friendly, because in many cases, you may be the only person that is preventing their lives from being destroyed. Many youth will look to you as the example they need to follow, or as the parent who never was.

Co-Workers

Another important priority in your life as a youth pastor, should be your relationship with your senior pastor and your co-workers in youth ministry (we will take a more detailed look at this in a later chapter). No youth ministry can go very far if the senior pastor does not see what you see, or understand your vision. You are an under shepherd and are thus under the authority and care of the pastor. Make sure your pastor shares your vision and understands what you are doing. Communication should always be open and clear, both written and oral.

Equally as important, is the relationship you have with your co-workers. These people who work with you must also see what you see, and be enthused enough about your vision to assist you in carrying it out. Communication is the key to success in this area.

Chapter 3

INGREDIENTS FOR SUCCESS

GOOD TEACHING

The bedrock of any youth ministry or any other ministry for that matter, must be the teaching of the word. The Bible states that ..."My people are destroyed because of a lack of knowledge" (Hosea 4:6). This is as true among young people as it is among adults.

Whatever is being taught at your church should be taught to your youth in a manner that they can easily understand and appreciate. This teaching should let teenagers know and understand the fundamental principles of the Christian faith, and should reflect much of what is being taught by the senior pastor to the adult members of your church.

Teaching your youth however, must be innovative and on a level which they can understand and relate to. Young people appreciate teaching that contains examples they can relate to.

The presentation must be different. In addition, you must teach about things that are of utmost concern to them. Teenage issues must be addressed. In today's world topics like AIDS, sex, abortion, family problems, violence, drugs, careers, college, music, entertainment and peer pressure must all be covered in a way they can relate to. Use interactive teaching. Get them involved or they will tune you out.

Your teaching must be much more exciting than what would be presented in a regular church service. The teenagers attention span is shorter and they are going through a phase where they have a need for fun, involvement and excitement. It is important to use examples and to involve them in the teachings. If you have difficulty in coming up with your own lesson plans, there are a number of youth oriented magazines and books that cover planning for youth Bible studies and youth meetings. Your local Christian bookstore should be able to assist you in locating these resources.

FELLOWSHIP AND RECREATION

The term "youth" implies a higher energy level, an exploring mind, and an idealistic nature. They are interested in trying new things, in having fun. Thus, young people need an outlet for their energies. They need to experiment in order to help them determine their future course in life. This means opportunities must be provided for them to explore, to interact with their peers, to engage in wholesome activities, which both expend energy and stimulate the whole man. Youth meetings should be considered by your youth a time of excitement, a "happening" place.

Your regular youth meetings should be exciting and should include activities that complement the teachings, but there must also be special events that your youth can look forward to. Many times in our youth meetings (Live Youth) there are ice breakers, skits that the kids are involved in, games and even wholesome pranks that get a point across.

Young people need a means to interact socially, to get to know one another, to make friends and to have an incentive to come to church on a regular basis.

Fun and recreational events often stimulate kids to want to become involved in other activities. Many times, my young people have said to me that they decided to come to our meetings on a regular basis after attending one of our talent shows, or beach parties or fun nights.

I believe that every church should have a gymnasium or some sporting facility for kids to play in. If we don't offer them some place to play, they will often play on the street or in a park run by dope dealers and gangs.

Some of the activities you may choose to hold include; sporting events such as a beach volleyball tournament, a three on three basket ball tournament, special movie or video nights where an exciting movie or video is shown. Talent shows are always good, because they help kids to discover their own talents and to be creative. Sometimes, you may also discover talents in your teens that you didn't know existed.

Another big event for us has been what we call 'Operation Burnout,' an all night affair, full of fun and activities that help them to expend energy and get the word in the process. You can be creative and come up with your own ideas or subscribe to Christian youth magazines which are full of ideas (e.g. Group Magazine, Fire by Nite, etc.) Find out what is fun for them and go for it.

Summer Camps or youth retreats can also serve the dual purpose of fun and spiritual growth.

PRAYER

Most teenagers are not likely to know all there is to know about prayer. In fact, when many of us think about prayer we think of some old ladies at a prayer meeting, dressed in white and crying all night for God to hear them.

Kids need to know that prayer is a responsibility, and that the Bible teaches we are all supposed to pray daily as a part of our relationship with the Lord.

We must teach the truth about prayer and let our young people know that prayer is one of the foundations for success in the life of any Christian, no matter what age.

One thing we need to teach about prayer is that it is not a chore. There are times when we should pray alone, other times when we pray as a group and sometimes when we pray with music as was done in the Old Testament (II Chronicles Chapter 5). Prayer should be both personal and group oriented. Young persons must be taught that prayer is not a thing you do when you become adult. Young people should be taught to pray for one another.

Many times in my meetings I ask them to pray for the person next to them, or have the whole group lay hands on one who has indicated a need. This helps to take the fear out of praying. Another thing I do is to ask them to pray at the beginning of meetings, for the offering, and at various other times. Many times, I do not tell them ahead of time and I often spread it around so that everyone feels that they can pray.

All youth should feel that prayer is an essential ingredient to a successful future and relationship with God. In addition to personal prayer time, you should also have times of group prayer for your teens.

All workers and youth leaders should set the example by praying themselves. If you are the youth pastor or a youth leader, you should pray for the kids in your group on a regular basis. You should also have a consistent life-style of prayer and fasting. Organized prayer meetings and times of fasting as a group, for both leaders and your entire youth group, are important.

DYNAMIC PRAISE AND WORSHIP

In as much as prayer is an important ingredient, so is praise and worship. No youth group can be successful without it. Praise and worship should be dynamic and exciting to your youth. It might be helpful to have someone other than yourself (unless you are musically inclined) responsible for worship. It is good to have one of your leaders devoted to and responsible for praise & worship. Some of your youth can also assist in this responsibility, if they possess musical abilities.

Praise and worship should be organized and skillful, and should be exciting. The same type of praise that you may use in a regular Sunday morning service may not be the best thing for your youth meeting. Develop a praise and worship team that is exciting and fun, and that your youth like. Whenever you find youth with special talents it is important to use them. It will help them to develop and gain confidence, and it will be a plus for you, as you will not have to do everything yourself.

Young people need to be given responsibility that will help them to feel like a part of your future plans. One day some of them will take your position, so why not help them to get started now in identifying their talents and using it for the Kingdom of God. To have your own praise band is a major plus to any youth group.

OUTREACH / EVANGELISM

Any group that does not look beyond its membership, will ultimately spend excessive time babysitting the aches and pains of group members. By focusing attention on the fact that each young person is called by God to go into their world and to reach others, less attention needs to be focused on the many temporal needs individual young people may face. Outreach should be done collectively and on an individual basis by members of your group. Effective group and personal outreach must be planned and executed with purpose.

As a youth leader, you will definitely not reach youth by yourself.

The book of Ephesians tells us that pastors, evangelists, teachers and so on are there to build up and equip the body to do the work of the ministry. We are to equip our youth so that they will in turn go out and reach their friends and family members. (Ephesians 4:9-11)

It is important to be creative. Witnessing is fun and in fact, whether you are a Christian or not, you witness everyday. MTV is a tremendous witnessing tool, only they are not preaching our message. Use what works in a given situation. Witnessing must be seen as fun, because it is. It is also work, but it can be fun in the process.

Teenagers will reach teenagers. You cannot do it alone. In fact, the majority of the work should be done by the teens themselves. They must tell their friends at school, they must convince their parents, they must invite their friends to church, they must be involved in missions or they will become dull and introverted.

At one time, I had kids in my group design their own tracts that they would give to their friends. It is amazing what they came up with.

Sometimes we may need to change our strategy. What may have worked during the "Jesus movement" twenty years ago may not work now. Come up with your own ideas.

Some of the things we have done are: Pass out tracts on the street, take a live band into a park, use drama in the park or in the city or even shopping malls. It is important to pray before, during and after organized outreaches, because we are in a war and our weapon of warfare is prayer, to combat forces that oppose us.

Do not be confined to a method, use whatever works. The Gospel is a message and not a method. Jesus said go into all the world, but he didn't say how.

Whatever type of evangelism you do, make sure you have a follow- up plan. Take the names, addresses and telephone numbers of the people you witness to, and add them to your mailing list. Have volunteers call them for counseling or invite them to church. Check on them periodically to insure that they are OK. Have some follow -up cards printed to record information correctly and keep the information in your computer if you have one.

Schools

Another important point of outreach is the Schools. More teenagers are in school than any-place else, so we must be in the schools. In some countries, they do not allow you to talk about God in the schools. But in our country (Bahamas), we have no such problem. At every opportunity we go into schools with special music, drama and exciting teachings.

If you live in a country where you are not allowed to use the name of Jesus, wisdom and tact are important. In one case, it may be expedient for you to become more militant and demand the right to be heard. In another case, you may want to use an anti-drug or "safe sex" campaign to get young people from a school to come and hear you later at a church.

It is vitally important to use the music they like, otherwise they often will not listen. Christian Rock music or Rap music can be used as a tool to get their attention and for them to accept you. If you go to a school and they do not identify with you, they will not stop to listen to what you have to say. Be like Jesus, he talked about water when he met the woman at the well and he talked about fish when he met fishermen like Peter and John.

Use your kids to pass out literature like your newsletter or tracts they have personally designed for their friends. Have your teens wear Christian T-Shirts. Send your newsletter to the principal or have one of the kids give it to the principal . Tell your youth to ask for you to come into their school. Help them with the formation and organization of Bible clubs.

In reaching high schools we need to pray for open doors, get to know, the principal and teachers on a friendly basis, research each school you are to go into (to be adequately prepared) and remember to communicate formally with appropriate authorities.

Youth need to be taught constantly how to mix and not to blend. Jesus was everywhere and he mixed with all kinds of people. He never became like any of them. They became more like him.

Foreign Missions

Foreign missions is very important. There are many Youth oriented mission organizations that travel all over the world using drama, music and one on one street witnessing to reach others. Teen Mania is one organization that has a worldwide ministry using teenagers.

Youth With a Mission is another. The impact of a foreign mission trip on a young person's life is tremendous, and often results in an entirely new outlook on life for them. This is a part of what Jesus said when he commanded us go into all the world. We should reach out to those around us first of all, then to those far away (e.g. as the Bible states Judea, Samaria and to all the world).

EVIDENCES OF FAITH AND POWER

Although GOD'S power cannot be legislated, your youth must see in you a faith that believes

God can do the impossible. We are told by God to pray for the sick, pray for him to intervene in our affairs and to believe that if we have faith in him and he is our source, things will happen on this earth that are God's work and not man's. We have a promise from God that tells us, if we believe his word nothing is impossible.

We must exude this type of faith to our youth. They need to know that we are not playing, that God is real and we have direct access to him through prayer. Whenever your young people have needs, they should be encouraged to pray and believe God in line with what his word says. Whatever the problem, we should pray and believe and leave it up to God to demonstrate his power among us.

We cannot make God do anything, but we can act on what he said and have faith for his promises. Prove this to them through prayer, by the laying on of hands and other biblical methods during your regular meetings. This should also be stressed as important in each individual life. After all, if God is God, then he can and wants to demonstrate his power among us as stated in his word, and has been proven by those who have gone before.

INVOLVEMENT OF YOUTH IN PLANNING AND WORK OF YOUTH MINISTRY

Effective and lasting youth ministry cannot be carried out by adult leaders only. Young people must be given the opportunity to develop their talents and abilities, otherwise they will become dependent and sluggish and will not be able to take your place or assist you after they have graduated from the group. In order for them to feel like a part of the youth ministry and to not consider themselves spectators, they must participate in Ministry.

They are youth today, but they will be the leaders of tomorrow. It is imperative that they be involved in the planning of *their* ministry.

For starters, you should have your youth decorate the room you use for your meetings. This gives them a sense of pride and identity. Secondly, you should get their ideas on everything you do. They should be involved in things like setting up the meeting area, carrying boxes or equipment, doing manual or other tasks. As a leader, you should not be setting up chairs or doing other such tasks while your youth sit and wait for you to get things ready.

In planning your yearly calendar, in determining special events, in deciding on a type of music, it is important to get their ideas.

Get them to evaluate meetings, events, and whatever you do, so that they are not sitting there bored to death while you are not even aware that what you are doing is not of interest to them.

You are not to be governed by their ideas but you should get their ideas before you make decisions.

In my youth ministry, every year I have a planning meeting with group members. I ask them what they learned during the previous year, what they liked, didn't like and what they would like to see in the coming year. This creates a sense of unity and an 'Our' mentality rather than a 'They' mentality.

LOVE

You must love and care about the youth you work with. If you don't love them or really care, you should do something else, because they will notice it and react accordingly. If it ever becomes a chore to you or if you are ever in youth ministry only because you cannot find some more exciting area of ministry, then you should quit. A genuine love for youth is definitely a prerequisite for successful youth ministry.

Young people are different, they are excitable, energetic and they have a style that may be different from your own. Many times you must be a much more tolerant person to work with youth because they are prone to experiment and make mistakes.

Many people find it difficult to work with youth, but that has never been the case for me. I love working with young people. Love for young people may mean having them over to your house for dinner some days, attending events that are special to them (graduation, a big game or performance, etc.) or just having them hang out with you. Youth ministry is also time consuming. If you are impatient or do not have time for them, you are in the wrong ministry. If you are in youth ministry on your way to a more important ministry, you are in the wrong business.

DISCIPLINE

In the same way that love is important discipline is also important. You cannot be effective if your young people have no discipline. Many times the only place where they will have an opportunity to learn discipline is when they meet you. Many of our young people today grow up without parental discipline or proper attitudes to authority. If this is not checked, they will come into your youth ministry and carry on a pattern of disruption and destroy the morale and attitudes of the teens you are working with.

You must maintain discipline and give instruction to teens as to how they should carry themselves. There should be a set of rules that govern your meetings and ministry that is explained to your young people.

If they go against established rules, there should be penalties once you are sure that they were aware of their transgressions. This would not apply to visitors, although there are certain things you cannot permit even for visitors. It is important to insure that no one interferes with the purpose of your group or meeting.

There are several things you should note with regard to discipline.

1) Seating Arrangements

It is my belief that the best seating arrangement with youth no matter what size the group, is in a circular fashion. Many youth hide in the back rows when you have traditional seating, but with a circle you are one on one with each person. It is much easier to communicate face to face using this method (see example 3.1)

It is important for your youth leaders to be involved in stopping distractions before you have to deal with it while you are speaking, so they should sit interspersed throughout the group.

2) Attention Seekers

Those seeking attention may need to be given a task (i.e. read a scripture, pray,) to diffuse their strategy and put them on the spot (where they wanted to be anyhow). The best way to diffuse an attention seeker is to give them attention. Not necessarily the attention they planned on getting, but the kind of attention that will cause them to rethink their strategy and where they would end up feeling like they should try not to disrupt.

Contemporary Arrangement

Traditional Arrangement

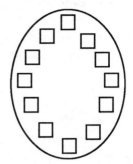

Example 3.1

3) Problem Persons

Sometimes you may run into young people whose express purpose is to be a problem, despite counselling or personal help from you. If you have such a 'problem person,' pull them aside or invite them to your office or home and have a talk with them. This often works wonders.

If they have no intention of doing things differently, you may need to send them home until they are ready to conform to simple rules. The important thing to remember is that God is a God of order, and you must help to teach youth order and discipline. If after trying you cannot get their cooperation, the best thing for both parties is that they find somewhere else to go. If a young person refuses to submit to your authority and leadership, they need to be elsewhere.

Chapter 4

Organization and Co-Ordination

ORGANIZATION IS THE KEY

Every youth ministry should have a blueprint, including where you are now, where you want to be a year from now and what you envision for your ministry in the future. No house is built without a blueprint.

Certainly God's youth ministry should not be developed "as it comes," there must be a plan, a vision that is written in definable terms, including how the ministry is to be organized, how meetings should be conducted and who will be responsible for what. Of course your plans can be adjusted and amended as necessary, but it is important to have a plan from which you can work and build on.

You should have all of the following as a part of your master planning:

- A statement of purpose
- Goals
- Objectives
- Cost
- Action plan
- An organizational chart
- Assignments of personnel
- Meeting plan
- Evaluation / monitoring

Shown below is an example of these items:

Live Youth Ministry - Master Plan

Scriptural Basis

...But I your servant have feared you Lord from my youth. I Kings 18:12

....For you are my hope, O Lord God, you are my trust from my youth. Psalm 71:5

TENANTS OF LIVE YOUTH:

- Word...the basis of every ministry
- Worship....God desires such, young or old
- Evangelism.....Go into all the world
- Fun....A focus of the Teen Years
- Power.....Based on the Holy Spirit
- Prayer.....for spiritual foundation

LIVE YOUTH

GOALS

1. To share the gospel of Jesus Christ to teen-agers in a way that they would be able to receive and relate to others.

2. To assist teens in their maturity through thought provoking examination of the word.

3. To assist teens in effective decision making and goal setting, enabling them to better deal with the issues that confront them.

4. To provide a social and recreational outlet for teens in an environment centered around the word.

5. To enhance the overall work of BFMF by careful incorporation of an exciting Youth Program into BFMF.

6. To develop a Youth Missions program b o t h home and abroad.

OBJECTIVES

A. To hold weekly "Friday Night Live" Bible teaching and Youth Training sessions.

B. To arrange regular times for "Spiritual Warfare" (i.e. prayer/fasting)

C. To establish a "Live Youth Praise Team" &"Music Ministry"

D. To implement monthly "Live Youth Home/School Turf" meetings (i.e. home/school Bible studies)

E. To organize a "Live Youth Drama Club"

F. To engage in "Live Youth City Swipes" (i.e. street witnessing)

G. To arrange Family Island/Overseas Missions

H. To host annual "Live Youth Camps/Conferences/Seminars"

I. To visit prisons, orphanages, hospitals etc.

J. To organize an Academic Assistance Network

K. To participate in Sunday/Friday Worship sessions (i.e. music, drama, sharing special youth Sundays & Fridays etc.)

L. To arrange "Live Youth Sunday Worship Sessions"

ACTION PLAN

1. Train and equip workers who would form a team that would orchestrate the BFMF "Live Youth" Youth Ministry. This would mean at-

tending workshops /seminars conducted by established youth ministries abroad, as well as at BFMF.

2. Establish times and schedules for meetings, special events, social and recreational activities, inclusive of a calendar of events for each year.

An example would be:

a) Regular Bible study/fun meetings held each Friday from 7:30-9:00 P.M..

b) Special events Friday/Saturday/Sunday nights ....An example of activities would be video concerts, live concerts,   boat cruises, one night or weekend/holiday retreats, special witnessing outings, sports days, prayer and praise meetings, etc.

Regular Meeting Format

7:30-7:50	Praise/Worship
7:50-8:05	Ice Breakers (getting to know each other)
8:10-8:20	Activities (drama, group disc.) or Special Music
8:20-8:50	Group word discussions/ Teaching.
8:50-9:00	Prayer/Alter Ministry

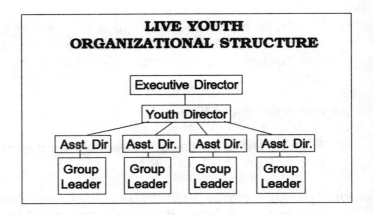

Directors Responsibilities:
- Care of group members
- Follow-up
- Planning of Events/Teachings etc.
- Participation in Services

Assistant Youth Directors will be responsible for:

- PRAISE & WORSHIP
- SPORTS
- TURF MEETINGS

- VISITATION/FOLLOW-UP
- MUSIC &DRAMA
- OUTREACH

JOB DESCRIPTIONS

EXECUTIVE YOUTH DIRECTOR is responsible for:

- Directing the vision of the Youth Group
- General oversight of the Youth Group
- Budgetary approvals
- Approval of program agenda
- Public Relations and promotion of activities

DIRECTOR is responsible to the EXECUTIVE DIRECTOR for:

- Implementation and achievement of goals and objectives
- Family Island and Overseas missions
- Membership and awards
- Weekly "Friday Night Live" meetings
- Academic Assistance Program
- Setting of program agenda
- Assigning youth members to each department

ASSISTANT DIRECTOR PRAISE & WORSHIP, MUSIC, DRAMA is responsible to the DIRECTOR for:

- Praise & Worship
- Live and recorded music
- Drama

**ASSISTANT DIRECTOR VISITATION &
HOME/School TURF/Live Youth Clubs
MEETINGS is responsible to The DIRECTOR
for:**

- Visitations (Prisons, Orphanages
  etc.)
- Live Youth Home/School (Live Youth Club)
  Turf Meetings
- Counselling and Street Witnessing training

**ASSISTANT DIRECTOR SPORTS &
RECREATION is responsible to the
DIRECTOR for:**

- Sporting activities
- Recreational Activities
- Games/Ice Breakers

**ASSISTANT DIRECTOR FUNDS & FINANCES
is responsible to the DIRECTOR for:**

- Setting budget
- Fund raising events
- Tithes/Offerings
- Purchasing (equipment etc.)

**ALL DIRECTORS WILL BE RESPONSIBLE
FOR:**

- Friday Night Live teaching and training ses-
  sions
- Youth Counselling
- Intercession & Fasting

- Oversight of Live Youth Groups/Clubs (Radicals/Club Dynamite ,etc.)
- Training of Youth Leaders (in Departments)
- Youth Director/Group Outings
- Substituting for fellow Youth Directors
- Attending monthly Youth Directors Meetings

PROPOSED BUDGET

PARTICULARS	Budget	Actual	Difference
INCOME			
Offerings	$0.00	$0.00	
Donations	$0.00	$0.00	
Book Sales	$0.00	$0.00	
Ticket Sales	$0.00	$0.00	
Other	$0.00	$0.00	
Product Sales	$0.00	$0.00	
Total Income	**$0.00**	**$0.00**	**$0.00**
EXPENDITURE			
Newsletter	$0.00	$0.00	
Events Costs	$0.00	$0.00	
Promotions	$0.00	$0.00	
Personnel	$0.00	$0.00	
Media	$0.00	$0.00	
Supplies	$0.00	$0.00	
Equipment	$0.00	$0.00	
Mail	$0.00	$0.00	
Transportation	$0.00	$0.00	
TOTAL EXP	$0.00	$0.00	$0.00
NET INCOME/LOSS	**$0.00**	**$0.00**	**$0.00**

SET CLEARLY DEFINED GOALS

The goals you set should be clearly defined. If your goal for this year is to see your group grow from 10 members to 25 members, this should be stated. If your goal is to win 100 youths for the Lord or whatever it may be, it should be clearly defined. Your goal should never be as vague as "TO HAVE A GOOD YEAR". Write down your goals in a manner which will enable you to obtain important information easily when you or others need it.

In addition to your goals, there should be a checklist to monitor your progress and a division of labor that indicates who will do what. One of the worst positions to be in is to be expecting something to be done, and the person you expect to do it does not know. Make sure you put names to tasks.

Here's an example of goals laid out for a Youth Conference we staged for several years called "Youth Alive."

GOALS

1.   Provide teaching to our youth that is relevant to their situation, with a focus on how to live a successful, well adjusted, Christian Life, countering the pervading negative youth trends of our society and world.

2.   Provide inspirational activities with a focus on music as a means of drawing youth to the

point where they can be confronted with the truth of the gospel.

3. Provide an outlet for youth on summer break from school that will be fun, wholesome and yet minister to the whole man.

TOPICS: "Youth & Parents." "Love, Sex and Dating," "Peer Pressure," "Developing a Positive Self Image" "The Big "AIDS" "Mean Green" "JC Homeys"...and other relevant material.

FORMAT

a) Four days and nights (July 6, 7, 8 & 9) of teachings (including special video presentations) covering topics mentioned above in special workshop sessions (days) and special evening sessions covering both teaching and limited special music.

b) Two days of concerts and activities (July 10th & 12th) beginning with an outdoor extravaganza July 10th, followed by a final concert indoors to wrap up "Youth Alive '92."

Expected Attendance/Focus:

Nightly meetings 300-500 per night. (Teaching, building up)
Outdoor event 2000 - 3000 (Entertainment, Inspiration, Salvation)

ARTISTS/SPEAKERS: Soldiers For Christ, Lester Lewis, FAIREST HILL, SYSTEM 3 , BFM MUSIC DEPT. , BFM YOUTH DEPARTMENT (Drama Team), OTHER SPIRIT FILLED LOCAL CHURCH YOUTH MINISTERS.

PERSONNEL ASSIGNMENTS

Item	Status	Who	Comments
Facility	booked	DB	get back to them on reception/food/picnic
Budget	not com	DAK	I need to work
Speaker letters	not com	DB	need to call local prospective speakers
Technical	in process	DB	discuss further with Andy
Printing	in process	DB	need to do concert poster
Public Relations	in process	DB	work with tech on ad's/get on radio & TV
Churches	nothing	DB	send out letter & schedule meeting/working on this
Program	in process	DB	need to assign topics etc.
Arrangements	nothing	DB	write speakers/artists/ compile information form
Promotions	nothing	DAK	discuss with DAK or check into with Pastor Myles etc.
T Shirts	nothing	Terri	talk to Terri about this
School Letters	completed	DB	done just need to be sent out
School Concerts	in process	DB	talk to Jasmine further
Police Presence	nothing	TB	talk to Tellis/Jay about this

USE A CALENDAR AND FILING SYSTEM

You should establish for yourself and your youth a calender of events on a year to year basis, updating it as necessary during the course of the year. This allows for continuity and helps you to avoid waking up in the night wondering what to do next. It also provides for your youth a sense of anticipation if they know what is planned during the course of the year. They may be able to schedule or re-schedule conflicting activities, vacations or other events if they know of the group activities ahead of time.

Make sure your youth help you plan your calendar. It is also important to plan with their input or consideration for things such as exams, important sports or social activities.

Of equal importance is the use of a filing system to keep records accurately and to ensure that information is easily accessible. If you have access to a computer this is a big plus. Computers can significantly contribute to productivity and organization. In addition, computers are great for producing newsletters, flyers, posters, budgets and so on.

You should also have a daily and monthly schedule. An organized "things to do" list is important, along with an appointment book. Schedule everything you do or you will find yourself busy, but not effective. To be effective, you need to maximize your time. Don't just say, "drop in whenever you have time," to someone you need to meet with. Give them an appointment.

Keep a calendar on your wall and mark important dates so as to avoid conflicts in scheduling. If you don't plan your time, someone else will plan it for you, someone who has no idea of the your priorities in life.

If you develop a schedule, adhere to it as much as possible and if you find it impossible, change it. Make sure your schedule reflects the priorities in your life (if playing basketball is not a high priority, then you need not have it scheduled five days a week).

PLAN TOMORROW TODAY

Always think of tomorrow. If one of your workers is leaving for a three month course, begin planning who is going to take his or her place. Do not wait until the worker is gone, then wonder what to do next. Plan the topics you will cover in your meetings for the next two months or six months or even the next year, plan the interaction you will use, plan the meeting format you will use. Always plan ahead. It is important to have an equipment plan so that you don't wait until the last minute and when you need your equipment, your financial department says to you, "but we had no idea you needed this."

USE MEETINGS WISELY

Plan your meetings at times and places that are convenient. You may even try to accomplish more than one goal with a meeting. For example, several of our youth department meetings have been held at the home of one of the youth leaders, and used as a time of socializing and fellowship after the meeting.

Time is precious, so meet if it is necessary and when it is necessary. Many times consuming meetings can be avoided by proper delegation of responsibilities to assistants, and the use of a simple phone call to check on the progress of the matter under concern. Meet only as often as necessary for the smooth functioning of the ministry.

One of the most effective methods of meeting that we have been able to establish, is a weekly planning meeting necessary for our youth department. We have an agenda and discuss the items that are important and relevant before any general discussion. At the end of the meeting, we spend some time praying for the youth and the needs of the ministry. The meeting is normally held at 6:00pm so that most of the workers can be home by 7:30pm. They come to the meetings directly after work, which means they do not have to go home and come out again. There are times when some persons cannot make it, and in such cases they stop by or call to get filled in on what went on during the meeting.

WRITE THINGS DOWN

Whenever giving instructions or keeping a record of events, make sure that each instruction is written down and both parties involved have copies of the correspondence. This avoids confusion and allows easy detection and resolution of problems that may arise.

Never get caught in the position of "But I thought you said you would be there at 11:00, not 3:00." Keep written records of your meetings, attendance, offerings and other pertinent data. This allows you to go back and better plan and evaluate. If you have no written records, you have no history on which to build on, or you will not know which bill to pay.

MAKE SURE YOU HAVE ENOUGH CAPABLE ASSISTANTS

No youth ministry, or any other ministry for that matter, can function with only one person who drives the bus, leads the worship, teaches, organizes the food line, etc. Make sure that your plan for ministry includes able assistants to whom you can delegate authority and responsibility.

One assistant may be responsible for the room set up, another for checking in at the bowling alley for an event, and another for supervising of skits or prayer times. The youth pastor should not normally drive the bus or be responsible for the set up work.

NORMALLY THERE SHOULD BE ONE WORKER FOR EVERY TEN YOUTH.

Examine workers to ensure that they are faithful before giving them responsibility. Find out their heart, their desires, their dreams, their character and their talents. Bring out the best in them by training them yourself, and by assisting them in receiving training at seminars outside your fellowship.

Many times, what I do with prospective leaders is allow them to come to the meetings, observe and participate for several months before giving them any responsibility. After this time, I sit with them and ask them how they feel about everything and help them make decisions based upon realistic expectations. As noted earlier in the organization section, you should have a job description for each person and position you establish.

Chapter 5

Other Important Items

RELATIONSHIPS

1. Co-workers

One of the most important aspects of youth ministry is the maintaining of relationships with the youth of your group and your assistants. Time should be spent sharing your life with your assistants and finding out their dreams, goals and desires for the future. You should be friends as well as co-workers.

2. Youth

Time should be spent inviting your youth one by one, or in small groups to your home and the homes of your assistants, in order to become more acquainted with them and to learn more about their important concerns. Strong relationships are based on understanding, and knowledge will enhance every aspect of your ministry.

It also says that you care and you are interested in them. Many times I have invited the most disgusting and disorderly young persons into my home, and have found out that their attitudes have drastically changed after they get over the shock of being invited. Interact with your youth on a casual basis.

> **For many young people, the fact that you would invite them into your home for a meal and sit down and talk with them, may mean the difference between success and failure for them.**

Ask them about school, call from time to time, ask them to help you do work or clean up your office. Be friendly in context. You are not a teenager, but you can identify with them. Do not try to be one of them. You will lose their respect and make a fool of yourself.

3. Parents

Parents must be involved, or at least aware of what you are doing and must have confidence in you. If parents are not confident in your leadership and do not understand what you are trying to accomplish, they will not trust you and will end up frustrating whatever you are trying to accomplish with your youth.

Make sure they get copies of your newsletters and communications, and make sure they know in advance of events that are coming up that involve their children. You may even want to have special parent's events, where they participate with their children. Make sure you know who their parents are, and that you talk to them wherever possible on a formal and informal basis.

SENIOR PASTOR

Your senior pastor will not automatically understand your vision, so it is important to communicate and share what you are feeling and where you are headed. Get his agreement on your program before launching it, to avoid misunderstanding and possibly bad feelings. Here are some points to keep in mind in dealing with your Senior Pastor:

a) Make sure that there is a mutual commitment by both of you to each other's vision, and that there is agreement on the part of the senior pastor with your vision (How can two walk together if they don't agree).

b) Make sure you communicate both verbally and in writing. Submit all of your plans and projects to your senior pastor. Communication avoids surprises and disagreements. There should be regular meetings between the youth pastor and senior pastor in order to maintain the type of communication necessary for effective mutual ministry.

c)   There should be no competition between the youth pastor and the senior pastor for popularity or influence. Each has a special role to play that is unique.

d)   Comparisons should not be made between youth and senior pastors. They work in different roles and the roles should be complimentary.

e)   The senior Pastor should not dominate or Lord over the youth Pastor. God has placed the senior pastor in authority and has given him the youth pastor for the purpose of accomplishing a mutual vision for youth. The youth pastor should be given the freedom and confidence to operate in an environment of common goals and purpose.

PUBLIC RELATIONS

One of the most important, and sometimes overlooked areas of youth ministry is the area of promotions and public relations. Many young people are apathetic and a concerted effort must be made to attract them, or they will not become involved in a youth fellowship. Many come to church on a regular basis, but may not ever become involved in your program. Your youth program must be visible to both youth and adults, especially parents.

Many parents, pastors and general church members have a tendency to forget that youth exist, except when they cause trouble or one of them does something negative. Your youth group should have a part in your regular church services and special events. Their talents should be exposed to the larger fellowship to maintain an interest in what you are doing, and also to prepare them for the leadership roles they will assume in the future.

It is important to have a youth bulletin that keeps your young people and regular church membership aware of what is going on in the youth ministry. It is also important to send letters to parents and to have meetings that help parents, youth and others, in understanding what you are doing.

An important tool for informing people about your youth group, is the use of a simple monthly newsletter. A newsletter can inform and update on a monthly or quarterly basis. Your youth can take extra copies to school, and you can send your newsletter to other youth pastors, high schools or college administrators and others who may benefit from or have some relationship with your Youth Ministry.

It is important to have a mailing list so that your ministry goes beyond just your local church. Keep others informed. Promote your events and have other churches involved wherever possible. It is also important to advertise outside of your youth group, through a mailing list, local newspaper, TV or whatever means available to you and within your budget.

> **If you have something exciting to offer, you must package it and offer it to those who can benefit. People will not automatically find out about and become excited about participating in your ministry.**

MTV and other organizations promote and package their message in an attractive manner. They spare no expense in getting their product out. We must use discretion and act wisely, but we must let people know.

SPECIAL EVENTS

Although this point was mentioned earlier, it should be noted the special place of camps and retreats in the development of youth. Camps are important to youth ministry. Moses and the other Bible leaders were trained in the wilderness. Camps provide times when youth can do business with God free from the distraction of every day life.

A camp or retreat allows them to be with you for a concentrated period, during which time you can confront them regarding the important issues of their life. Make sure camps are well organized and you check out a camp site before planning a camp.

AVOIDING PITFALLS

One other important point to remember is that anyone who is in Christian ministry is in a war. We do have an enemy who tries to distract us and destroy what God has helped us to build. Here are some things you should keep in mind to help in avoiding those pitfalls.

Conduct:

i)   Always be careful to avoid questionable situations.

ii)   Never go to a young person's house to counsel, especially if they are home alone. Do your counselling in an open setting and include your spouse when dealing with the opposite sex.

iii)   Let ladies counsel young ladies and men counsel young men. If you are married, use your wife to counsel young ladies and vice versa.

iv)   Do not drive young ladies home late at night. If necessary invite a young man along and have him sit in the front seat.

v)   Never get physically or emotionally involved with your youth. Young ladies are naturally attracted to older men and young men are often attracted to older ladies. Help them to relate to you as a leader and not someone on their level of relationship.

vi)   Be careful how you touch members of the opposite sex. Make sure you do not do anything to give off wrong signals.

vii) Do not call members of the opposite sex except for specific work or ministry related projects.

viii) Make sure that you have competent male and female leaders working with you. Both are needed as every group will have both male and female members.

CONTEMPORARY ISSUES

Make sure you are aware of and informed about the pertinent issues of the day relative to youth. Aids, abortion, drugs, music, entertainment, and suicide among others, are issues you should be able to give biblical advice on and make intelligent comments about. Let's take music for example. It is not bad, it depends on the musicians and the words more than anything else. The music you suggest your youth to listen to should be wholesome and should point them to the Lord, no matter which style of music it is.

It is also important to check out the artists' life-style. Do not invite someone to perform or minister to your youth whose life-style does not back up what they sing.

There is much good in contemporary Christian music and there is much bad. Be aware of what's out there, good or bad so that you can give good advice. The same should apply to entertainment

CONCLUSION

I noted previously the importance of reaching today's youth. In many ways, the times we live in are trying times, especially for our youth. You are a light in the dark, you are the salt in a decaying and rotting world. Thousands of young people grope everyday in the wilderness of today's world, seeking truth, wanting for fathers, mothers and adults who care. They search everyday for role models and they find less and less. They look for answers to life's most difficult questions and are not given any. In the end, they kill themselves, because they discover that a condom is not the answer, an abortion is not the answer, violence is not the answer.

We are here, we have the answer but we must package, promote, organize and mobilize our re-sources for the saving of another generation headed for destruction. We can do it, we must do it, we will do it. Not everyone will understand, not everyone will come, but as Jesus was known to say........whosoever will, let him come......

Just Do It!.......DB

Talk to Me
by Dave Burrows

This book by "Live Youth" Director and Youth Pastor Dave Burrows of Bahamas Faith Ministries, is a book that asks and answers the questions often asked about teenagers, by teenagers. From the perspetive of the "Maker," this book focuses on the life issues that face teens, ranging from drugs to sex to parents to music to peer pressure. This book will help both teenagers and parents gain a new understanding on these age old issues. Written "in your face" by a man who knows what it is to be a troubled youth living in a world of violence, drugs and street culture. Price $4.95

Audio & Video Cassettes
by DAVE BURROWS

JC Homey's
Instructions From The Maker
Love, Sex & Dating. 4 - TAPES
Get Busy
Family Matters 1
Family Matters 2
Building a Youth Ministry
Redeeming the Time
It Be Slammin (Music Seminar
   with Fairest Hill & Lester Lewis).
Hormone High School
Youth & Parents Face to Face
Peer Pressure.
Effective Parenting
Forming & Defining Values
The Single Man
Developing a Positive Self Image
Youth & The Music Scene (with Steve Wiley)
Progress of the Plan
There is Peace
God's Attitude Towards Healing
Godliness is Profitable
Jesus the First & the Last

Audio cassettes $6.00 Video Cassettes $25.00

LIVE ACTION VIDEO CLUB

An exciting monthly video for individuals or youth groups. One hour of exciting music, interviews, drama and fun, hosted by Dave 'Davy B' Burrows and a variety of special guests, artists, authors and speakers. Non stop Video fun and inspiration. $20.00 per month or $200.00 per year plus $3.50 shipping & handling.

BOOKS BY David Burrows

Strategies for Saving the Next Generation $5.95
by Dave Burrows

This book will teach you how to start and effectively operate a vibrant youth ministry. This book is filled with practical tips and insight gained over a number of years working with young people from the street to the parks to the church. Dave Burrows offers the reader vital information that will produce results if carefully considered and adapted. Excellent for Pastors and Youth Pastor as well as youth workers and those involved with youth ministry.

Talk to Me $5.95
by Dave Burrows

A guide for dialogue between parents and teens. This book focused on the life issues that face teens, ranging from drugs to sex to parents to music to peer pressure. This book will help both teenagers and parents gain a new understanding on these age old issues. Written "in your face" by a man who knows what it is to be a troubled youth living in a world of violence, drugs and street culture.

BOOKS BY Dr. Myles Munroe:

Becoming A Leader	**$9.95**
Becoming A Leader Workbook	**$7.95**
How to Transform Your Ideas into Reality	**$7.95**
Single, Married, Separated and Life After Divorce	**$7.95**
Single, Married, Separated Workbook	**$7.95**
Understanding Your Potential	**$7.95**
Understanding Your Potential Workbook	**$6.95**
Releasing Your Potential	**$7.95**
Releasing Your Potential	**$6.95**
The Pursuit of Purpose	**$7.95**

OTHER BOOKS BY:

Richard Pinder, Pastor, Bahamas Faith Ministries, Derwin Stewart and Dr. Mensa Otabil.

Mobilizing Human Resources $7.95
by Pastor Richard Pinder

Pastor Pinder gives an in-depth look at how to organize, motivate and deploy members of the body of Christ in a manner that produces maximum effect for your ministry. This book will assist you in organizing and motivating your 'troops' for effective and efficient ministry. It will also help the individual believer in recognizing their place in the body, using their God given abilities and talents to maximum effect.

The Minister's Topical Bible $14.95
by Derwin Stewart

The Minister's Topical Bible covers every aspect of the ministry providing quick and easy access to scriptures in a variety of ministry related topics. This handy reference tool can be effectively used in leadership training, counseling, teaching, sermon preparation and personal study.

Four Laws of Productivity $7.95
by Dr. Mensa Otabil

In Genesis 1:28, God commanded man to do four things: (1) "Be fruitful, and (2) multiply, and (3) replenish the earth, and (4) subdue it: and have dominion .." In the past, many people read and thought that this scripture only meant to have many children. This scriptural passage is not confined to reproduction, but is the foundation for all productivity. The Four Laws of Productivity by Dr. Mensa Otabil will show you how to: Discover God's gift in you, develop the gift, and how to be truly productive in life. The principles revealed in this timely book will radically change your life.

Available at your local bookstore or from:

To order or to receive a free catalog call:

Pneuma Life Publishing
Toll Free
(800) 727-3218

Bahamas Faith Ministries
(809) 393-7700